ADVE

Snowdonia

Including part of Snowdonia National Park

■ Snowdonia is an area of great beauty with many places of interest and natural attractions.

■ This new publication contains Ordnance Survey 'Explorer' maps in a convenient book format with a useful index to the main attractions focusing on the northern part of the Snowdonia National Park. It is the essential companion when exploring, showing all footpaths, rights of way and public access land.

CONTENTS

Geographers' A-Z Map Company Limited

Fairfield Road, Borough Green,
Sevenoaks, Kent TN15 8PP
Telephone: 01732 781000 (Enquiries & Trade Sales)
01732 783422 (Retail Sales)
www.az.co.uk
Copyright © Geographers' A-Z Map Company Limited
EDITION 1   2012

This product includes mapping data licensed from Ordnance Survey® with the permission of the Controller of Her Majesty's Stationery Office.

Mapping contents © Crown copyright and database rights 2011 Ordnance Survey 100017302

Communications

ROADS AND PATHS
Not necessarily rights of way

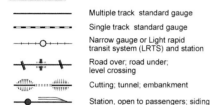

<S> Service Area	
7 Junction number	
M I or A 6(M)	Motorway
A 35	Dual carriageway
A 30	Main road
B 3074	Secondary road
	Narrow road with passing places
	Road under construction
	Road generally more than 4m wide
	Road generally less than 4m wide
	Other road, drive or track, fenced and unfenced
>> >	Gradient: steeper than 20% (1 in 5); 14% (1 in 7) to 20% (1 in 5)
Ferry	Ferry; Ferry P – passenger only
	Path

RAILWAYS

	Multiple track standard gauge
	Single track standard gauge
---O---	Narrow gauge or Light rapid transit system (LRTS) and station
	Road over; road under; level crossing
	Cutting; tunnel; embankment
	Station, open to passengers; siding

PUBLIC RIGHTS OF WAY

---------- Footpath	------- Bridleway
+++++++ Byway open to all traffic	
-+-+-+-+-	Restricted byway (not for use by mechanically propelled vehicles)

Public rights of way shown on this map have been taken from local authority definitive maps and later amendments. Rights of way are liable to change and may not be clearly defined on the ground.
Please check with the relevant local authority for the latest information.

The representation on this map of any other road, track or path is no evidence of the existence of a right of way.

OTHER PUBLIC ACCESS

• • • Other routes with public access (not normally shown in urban areas)

The exact nature of the rights on these routes and the existence of any restrictions may be checked with the local highway authority. Alignments are based on the best information available.

National Trail /

Long Distance Route

Recreational Route

--- --------- Permissive footpath

— — — — Permissive bridleway

Footpaths and bridleways along which landowners have permitted public use but which are not rights of way. The agreement may be withdrawn.

• • • Traffic-free cycle route

1 National cycle network route number – traffic free

1 National cycle network route number – on road

DANGER AREA — Firing and test ranges in the area. Danger! Observe warning notices

Visit www.access.mod.uk for information

ACCESS LAND

Portrayal of access land on this map is intended as a guide to land which is normally available for access on foot, for example access land created under the Countryside and Rights of Way Act 2000, and land managed by the National Trust, Forestry Commission and Woodland Trust. Access for other activities may also exist. Some restrictions will apply; some land will be excluded from open access rights.
The depiction of rights of access does not imply or express any warranty as to its accuracy or completeness. Observe local signs and follow the Countryside Code.

Visit www.ccw.gov.uk for up-to-date information

	Access land boundary and tint
	Access land in woodland area
🛈	Access information point
MANAGED ACCESS	Access permitted within managed controls for example, local bylaws

Visit www.access.mod.uk for information

General Information

BOUNDARIES

— -+- -+- —	National
— · — · — · —	County (England)
— — — — —	Unitary Authority (UA), Metropolitan District (Met Dist), London Borough (LB) or District (Scotland & Wales are solely Unitary Authorities)
· · · · · · · · · · · ·	Civil Parish (CP) (England) or Community (C) (Wales)
	National Park boundary

VEGETATION
Limits of vegetation are defined by positioning of symbols

Coniferous trees			
Non-coniferous trees			
Coppice			
Bracken, heath or rough grassland		Orchard	
Marsh, reeds or saltings		Scrub	

GENERAL FEATURES

+   Place of worship

Current or former place of worship

●   with tower

●   with spire, minaret or dome

□ ▢   Building; important building

▨   Glasshouse

▲   Youth hostel

■   Bunkhouse/camping barn/other hostel

⬣   Bus or coach station

Ж Ж Ж   Lighthouse; disused lighthouse; beacon

△ Ⱶ   Triangulation pillar; mast

✗   Windmill, with or without sails

Ⱦ Ⱦ   Wind pump; wind turbine

pylon   pole   Electricity transmission line

||||||||||||| Slopes

Gravel pit   Sand pit

Other pit or quarry   Landfill site or slag/spoil heap

BP/BS	Boundary post/stone
CG	Cattle grid
CH	Clubhouse
FB	Footbridge
MP ; MS	Milepost; milestone
Mon	Monument
PO	Post office
Pol Sta	Police station
Sch	School
TH	Town hall
NTL	Normal tidal limit
W; Spr	Well; spring

HEIGHTS AND NATURAL FEATURES

52 ·   Ground survey height

284 ·   Air survey height

Surface heights are to the nearest metre above mean sea level. Where two heights are shown, the first height is to the base of the triangulation pillar and the second (in brackets) to the highest natural point of the hill.

☐   Water

▨   Mud

▨   Sand; and & shingle

Vertical face/cliff

75
60
50

Contours may be at 5 or 10 metres vertical interval

Loose rock   Boulders   Outcrop   Scree

ARCHAEOLOGICAL AND HISTORICAL INFORMATION

✤   Site of antiquity

⚔ 1066   Site of battle (with date)

✳ ▦   Visible earthwork

VILLA   Roman

Castle   Non-Roman

Information provided by English Heritage for England and the Royal Commissions on the Ancient and Historical Monuments for Scotland and Wales

Selected Tourist and Leisure Information

P   Parking

P&R   Park & Ride, - all year

P&R   - seasonal

ℹ   Information cen. - all year

ℹ   - seasonal

V   Visitor centre

⚑   Forestry Commission visitor centre

National Park Information cen.

PC   Public convenience

✆   Telephone - public

✆   - roadside assistance

✆   - emergency

Å   Camp site

⛟   Caravan site

Ⓚ   Recreation leisure sports centre

⚑   Golf course or links

Theme pleasure park

🚂   Preserved railway

🍺   Public house/s

Craft centre

❗   Walks/trails

🚲   Cycle trail

Mountain bike trail

🚲   Cycle hire

U   Horse riding

Viewpoint

✕   Picnic site

Ⲯ   Country park

Garden arboretum

Water activities

Slipway

Boat trips

Boat hire

Nature reserve

Fishing

☆   Other tourist feature

✝   Cathedral/Abbey

ⅿ   Museum

Castle/fort

Building of historic interest

HC   Heritage centre

National Trust

Cadw (Welsh heritage)

◈   World Heritage site/area

Scale 1:25 000

1 Kilometre = 0.6214 mile
1 metre = 3.2808 feet

1 mile = 1.6093 kilometres
100 feet = 30.48 metres

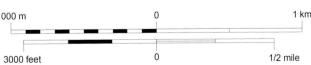

1000 m   0   1 km

3000 feet   0   1/2 mile

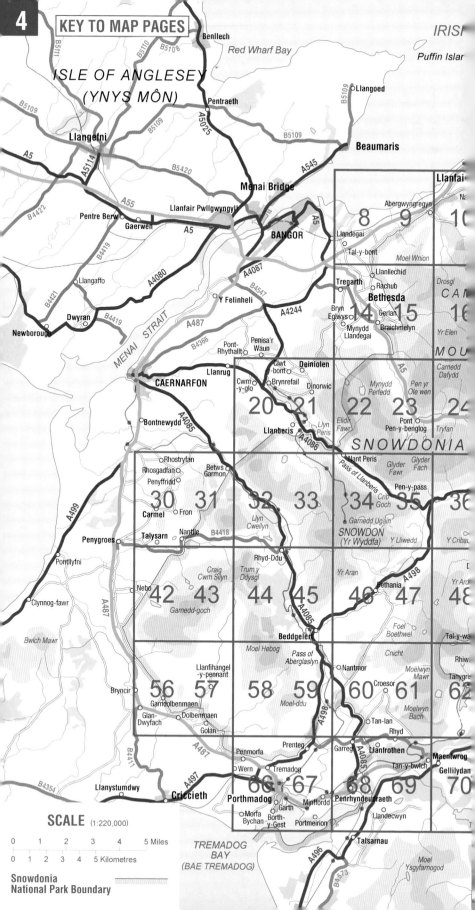

4

ISLE OF ANGLESEY
(YNYS MÔN)

IRISH

Red Wharf Bay

Puffin Islar

B5111
B5110
B5108
Benllech

Llangoed

B5109
B5109
Pentraeth

A5025

Llangefni

B5420

B5109

Beaumaris

A5114

A5

A55

A545

Menai Bridge

B4422

Llanfair Pwllgwyngyll

Llanfai

Abergwyngregyn

8

9

10

Pentre Berw

Gaerwen

A5

BANGOR

Llandegai

Tal-y-bont

Moel Wnion

B4419

A4080

Llangaffo

A4087

Tregarth

Llanllechid

Rachub

Drosgl

CAN

B4421

Y Felinheli

B4547

Bethesda

Gerlan

16

Dwyran

B4419

A487

A4244

Bryn
Eglwys

14

15

Yr Elen

Newborough

B4366

Pont-
Rhythallt

Penisa'r
Waun

Mynydd
Llandegai

Braichmelyn

MOU

MENAI STRAIT

Clwt
y-bont

Deiniolen

Carnedd
Dafydd

CAERNARFON

Llanrug

Cwm-
y-glo

Brynrefail

Dinorwic

Mynydd
Perfedd

A5

Pen yr
Ole wen

Carnedd
Ugain

Bontnewydd

A4085

20

21

22

23

24

A4086

Llanberis

Llyn
Peris

Elidir
Fawr

Pont
Pen-y-benglog

Tryfan

SNOWDONIA

A499

Rhostryfan

Betws
Garmon

Nant Peris

Pass of Llanberis

Glyder
Fawr

Glyder
Fach

Pen-y-pass

Rhosgadfan

Penyffridd

30

31

32

33

34

35

36

Carmel

Fron

Llyn
Cwellyn

Crib
Goch

Garnedd Ugain

Talysarn

Nantlle

B4418

SNOWDON
(Yr Wyddfa)

Y Lliwedd

Y Cribau

Penygroes

Rhyd-Ddu

Yr Aran

Yr Ard

Pontllyfni

Nebo

Craig
Cwm Silyn

Trum y
Ddysgl

42

43

44

45

46

47

48

Clynnog-fawr

Garnedd-goch

Bethania

A498

A487

Bwlch Mawr

Beddgelert

Foel
Boethwel

Tal-y-wa

A4085

Moel Hebog

Pass of
Aberglaslyn

Cnicht

Rhiw

Bryncir

Llanfihangel
-y-pennant

Nantmor

Moelwyn
Mawr

Tanygris

56

57

58

59

60

61

62

Garndolbenmaen

Glan-
Dwyfach

Dolbenmaen

Moel-ddu

Croesor

Moelwyn
Bach

Golan

Tan-lan

Rhyd

B4411

A487

Prenteg

Garreg

Llanfrothen

Maentwrog

Llanystumdwy

A497

Penmorfa

Tan-y-bwlch

Gellilydan

70

B4354

Wern

Tremadog

66

67

68

69

Criccieth

Porthmadog

Minffordd

Penrhyndeudraeth

Morfa
Bychan

Garth

Mynffordd

Llandecwyn

Borth-
y-Gest

Portmeirion

Talsarnau

TREMADOG
BAY
(BAE TREMADOG)

A496

Moel
Ysgyfarnogod

B4573

SCALE (1:220,000)

0   1   2   3   4   5 Miles

0 1 2 3 4 5 Kilometres

Snowdonia
National Park Boundary

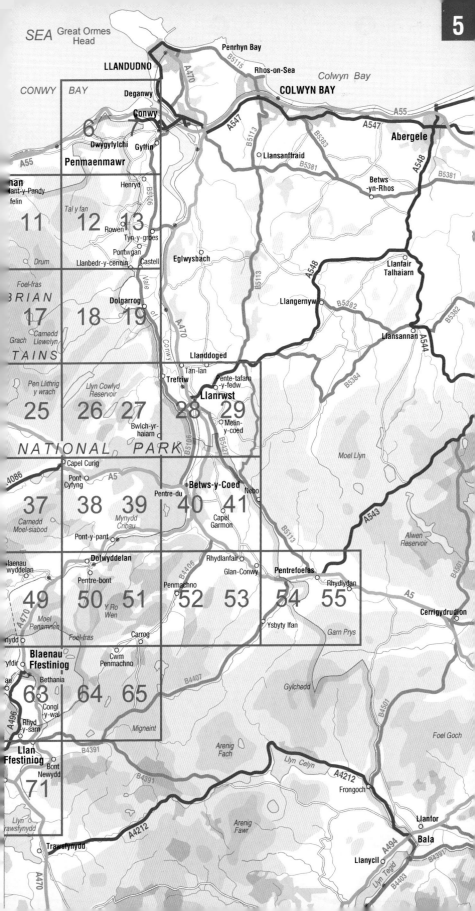

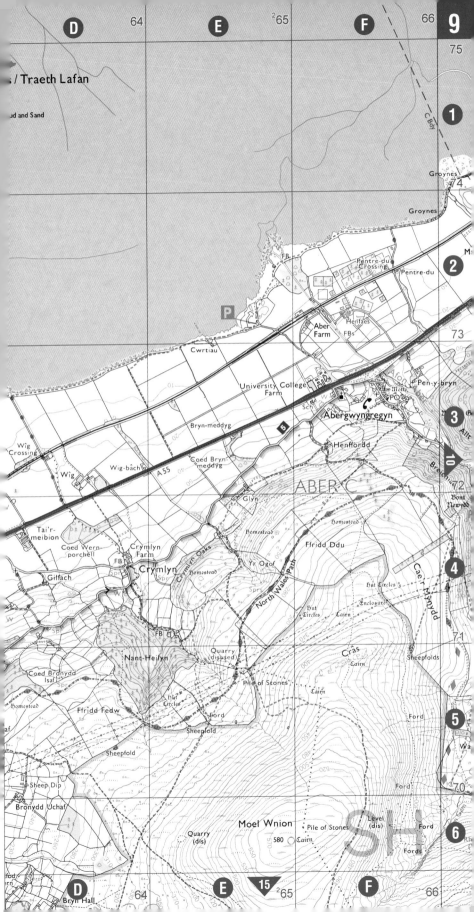

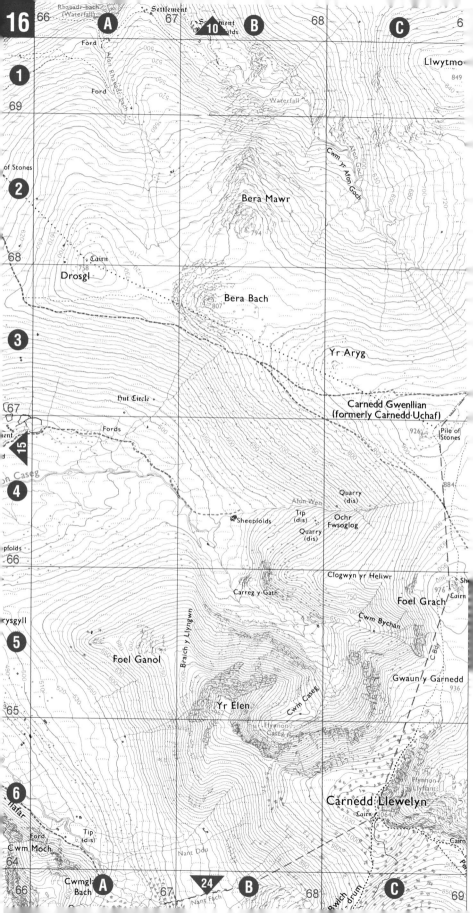

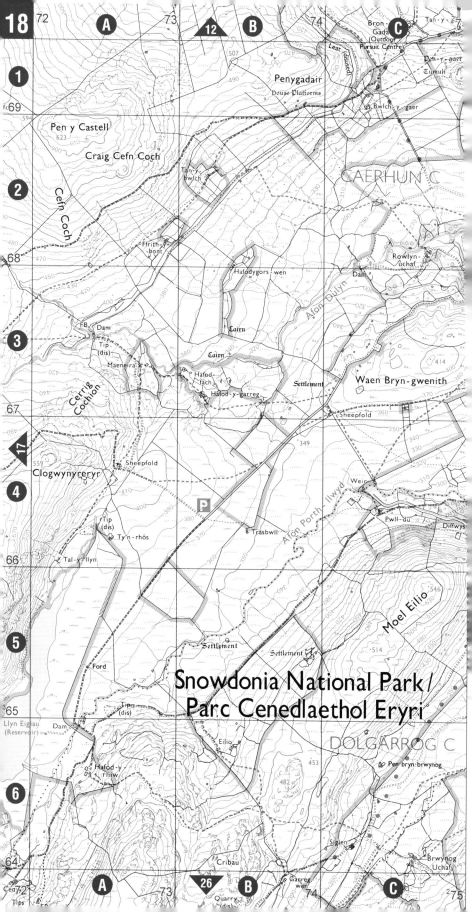

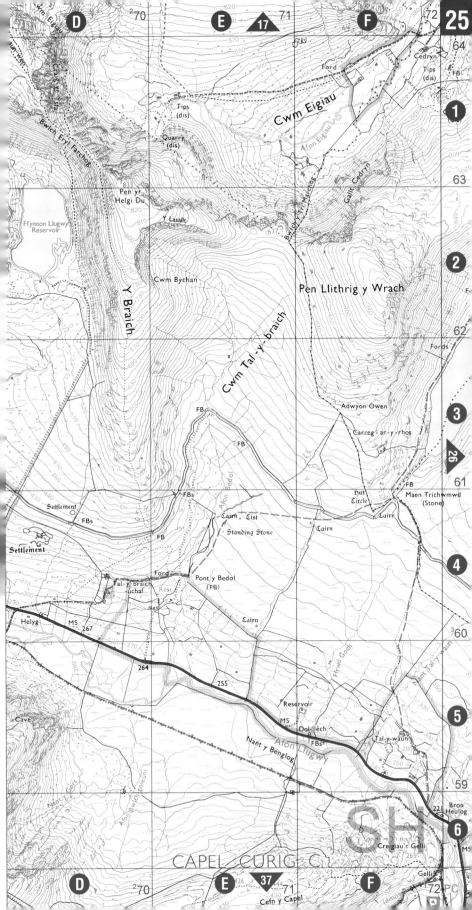

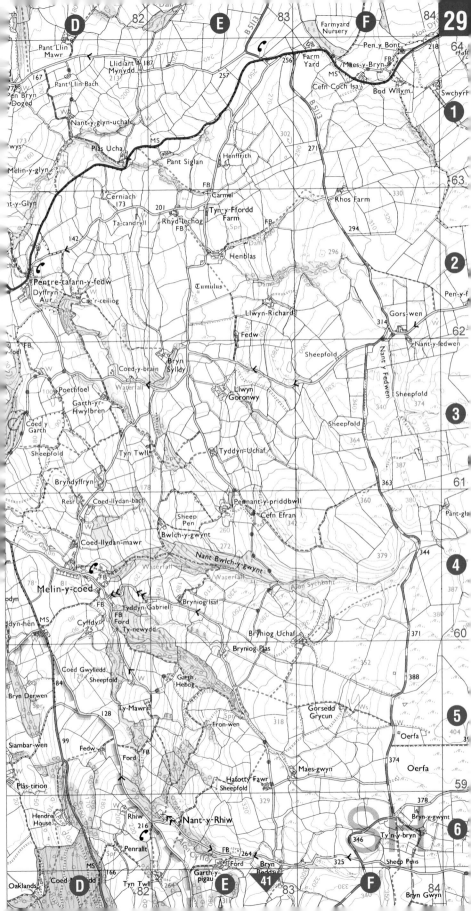

Snowdonia National Park/
Parc Cenedlaethol Eryri

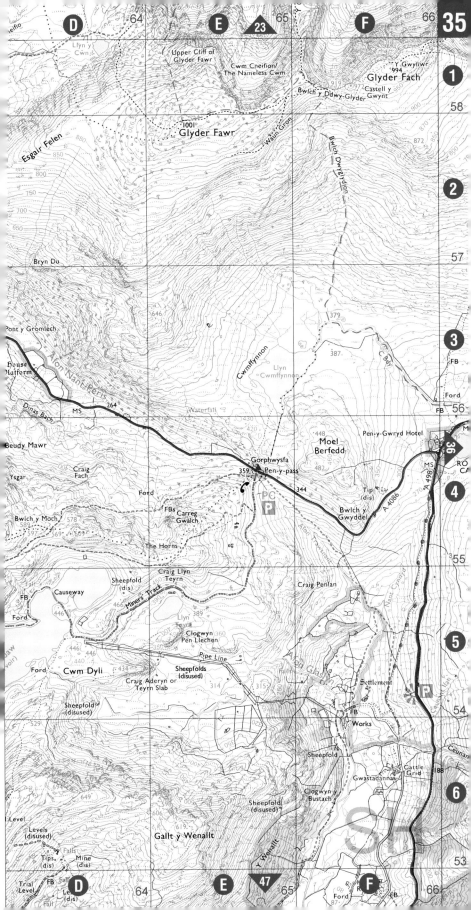

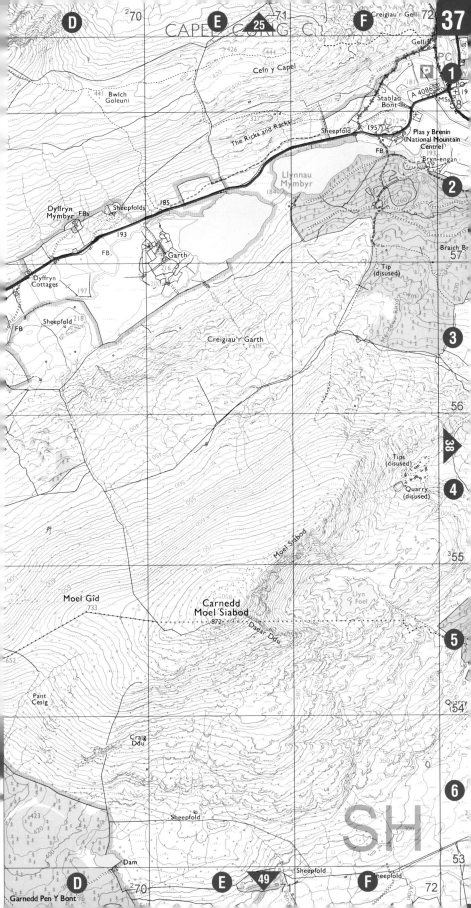

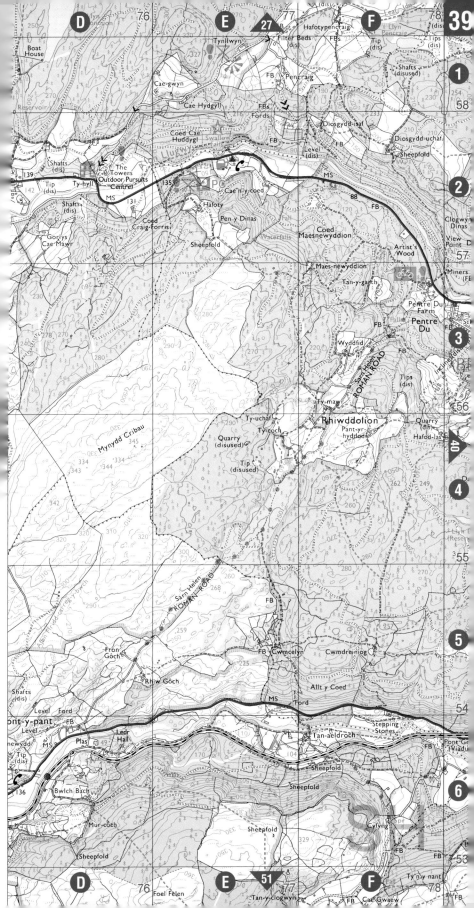

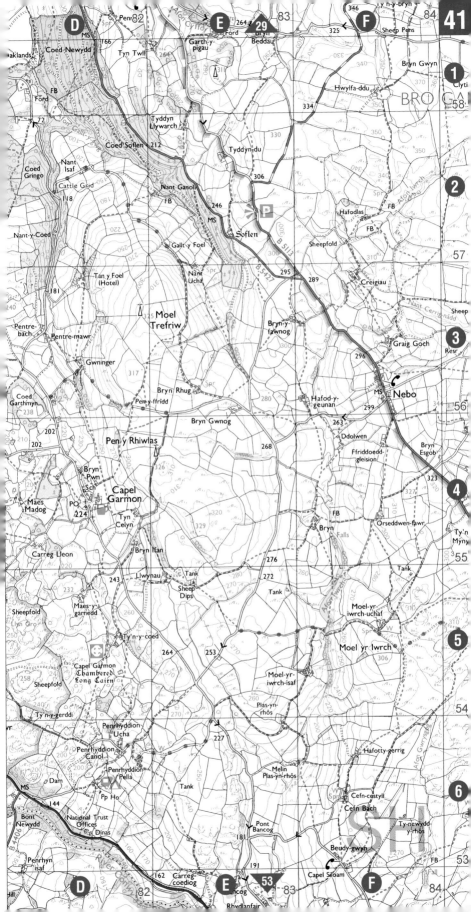

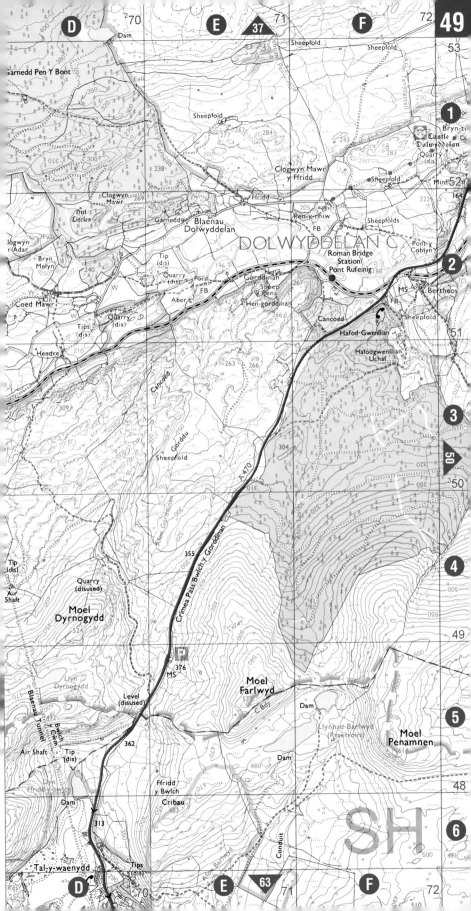

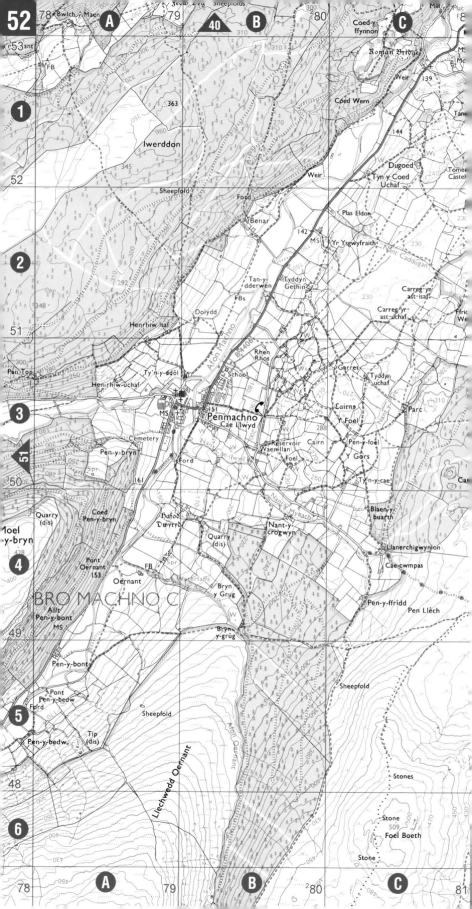

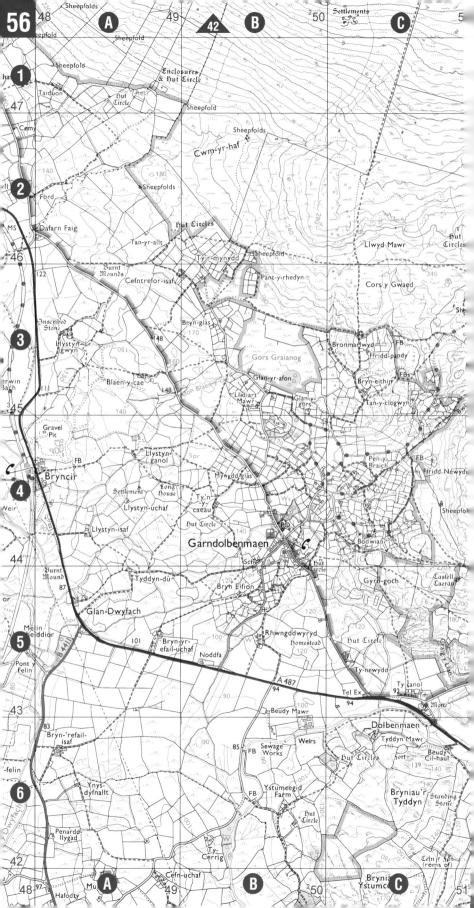

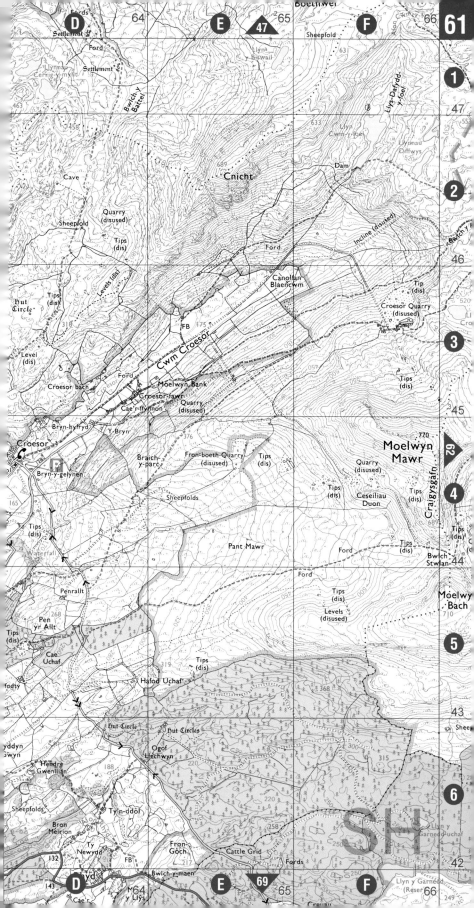

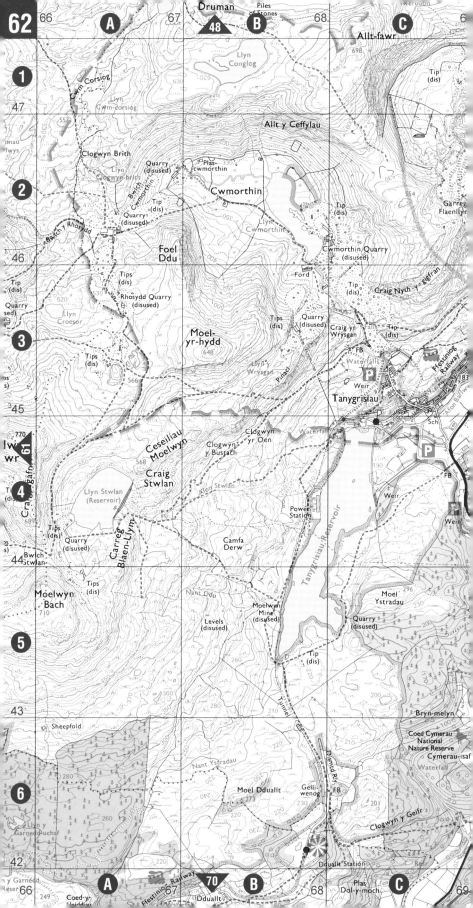

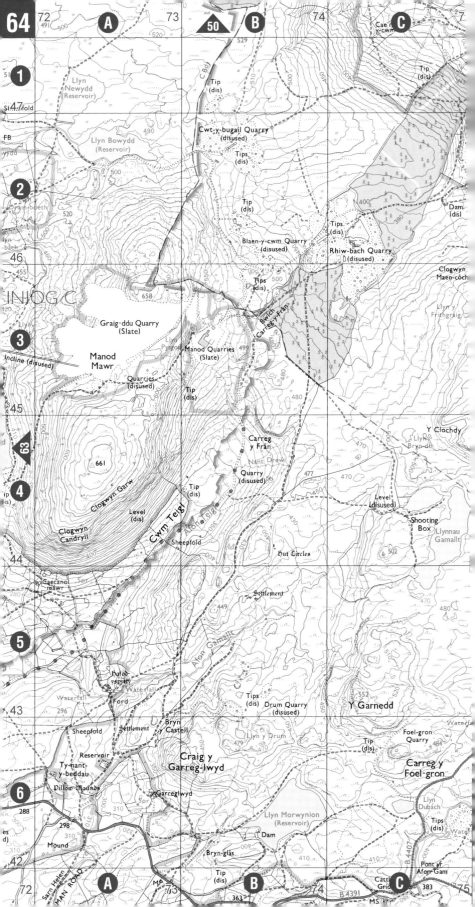

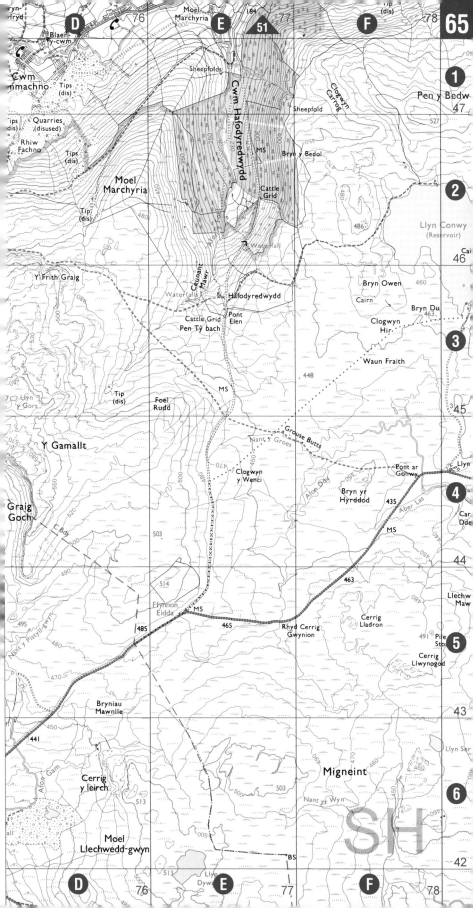

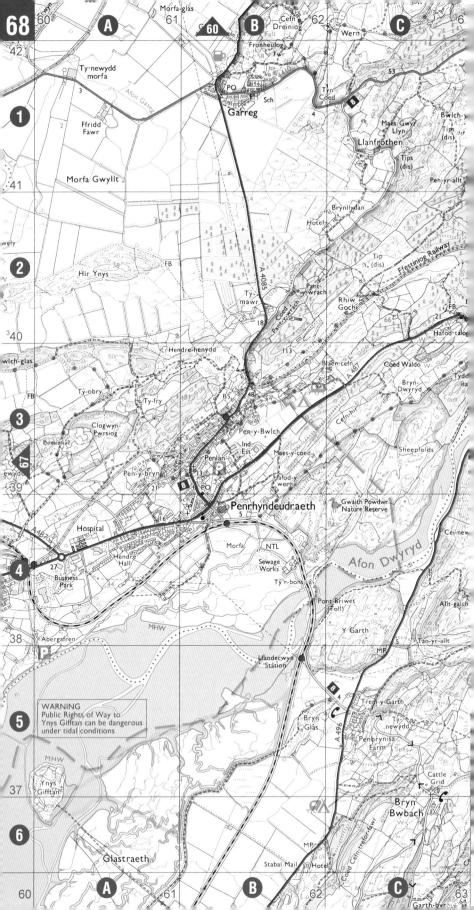

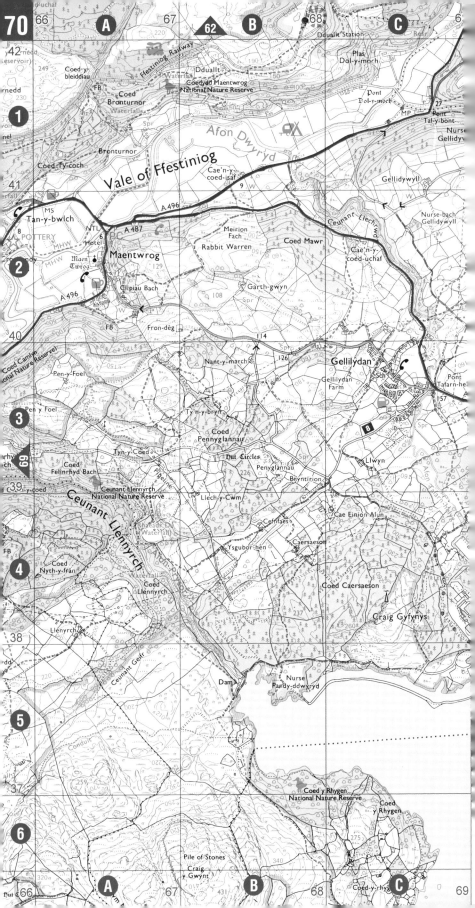

HOW TO USE THIS INDEX

1. The map reference given refers to the actual square in which the feature is located and not the name.

2. A strict alphabetical order is used e.g. Foelgraig follows Foel Grach but precedes Foel Gron

THE NATIONAL GRID REFERENCING SYSTEM

The grid lines form part of the National Grid and are at 1 km intervals.

To give a unique reference position of a point to within 100 metres proceed as follows:

Sample point: **Abergwyngregyn**

1. Read letters identifying 100,000 metre square in which the point lies (**SH**)

2. FIRST QUOTE EASTINGS - locate the first VERTICAL grid line to LEFT of the point and read the BLUE figures labelling the line in the top or bottom margin of the page (**65**). Estimate tenths from the grid line to the point (**6**). This gives a figure of **656**

3. THEN QUOTE NORTHINGS - locate the first HORIZONTAL grid line BELOW the point and read the BLUE figures labelling the line in the left or right margin of the page (**72**). Estimate tenths from the grid line to the point (**6**). This gives a figure of **726**

Sample Reference: **Abergwyngregyn SH 656 726**

raig Fach . . . . .4D 35   SH 635 556
raig-fawr . . . . .5D 17   SH 698 655
raig Ffynnon . . . . . .1A 26   SH 726 636
raig Gyfynys . . . . . .4C 70   SH 683 382
raig Hafodwen . . . .6B 6   SH 730 753
raig Isallt . . . . . . .3F 57   SH 531 450
raig Llugwy . . . . . .2C 24   SH 681 629
raig Llyn Teyrn . . . .5E 35   SH 641 549
raiglwyn . . . . .4B 26   SH 730 608
raig Nant Peris . . . .2C 34   SH 628 574
raig Nyth-y-gigfran . .3C 62   SH 685 458
raig Penlan . . . . . .5F 35   SH 651 548
raig Pennant . . . . .3E 43   SH 529 505
raig Tan-y-bwlch . . .4A 50   SH 728 492
raig Trum y Ddysgl . .2A 44   SH 544 519
raig Wen . . . . .4A 26   SH 729 602
. . . . .3F 45   SH 597 508
raig y Bera . . . . . .5A 32   SH 540 542
raig y Dulyn . . . . . .4D 17   SH 696 663
raigyfedwen . . . . . .5D 7   SH 754 762
raig-y-garn . . . . . .4D 57   SH 510 444
raig y Gesail . . . . . .1A 66   SH 543 412
raig y Llan . . . . . . .5C 56   SH 508 434
raig y Llyn . . . . . . .2C 24   SH 688 626
raig yr Ogof . . . . . .3D 43   SH 516 503
raig yr Ysfa . . . . . .1D 25   SH 693 637
raigysgafn . . . . . . .4F 61   SH 659 444
ras . . . . .5F 9   SH 653 709
Creigiau Gleision . . .2B 26   SH 733 622
. . . . .3D 23   SH 632 611
Creigiau Hiirion . . . . .2C 24   SH 683 625
Creigiau Malwod . . .2B 24   SH 672 625
Creigiau'r Garth . . . .3E 37   SH 706 564
Creuau . . . . .1F 69   SH 652 419
Cribau . . . . .5B 34   SH 616 542
Crib-Goch . . . . . . .4C 34   SH 624 552
Crib-y-Ddysgl . . . . .4B 34   SH 610 551
Crimea Pass . . . . . .4E 49   SH 702 493
Crimea Pass Car Park . .5E 49   SH 701 489
Crimpiau . . . . .5B 26   SH 733 595
Croesor . . . . .4D 61   SH 630 447
Crymlyn . . . . .4D 9   SH 638 715
Cwm Beudy Mawr . .4D 35   SH 630 558
Cwm Brwynog . . . .4F 33   SH 593 559
Cwm Bual . . . . . . .3D 23   SH 632 616
Cwm Bychan . . . . .2E 25   SH 701 623
. . . . .2A 60   SH 601 468
Cwm Caregog . . . .1F 45   SH 593 529
Cwm Cesig . . . . . .2C 32   SH 561 570
Cwm Ciprwth . . . .6E 43   SH 522 478
Cwm Clogwyn . . . .5F 33   SH 597 543
Cwm Clorad . . . . .4B 36   SH 679 554
Cwm Cneifio . . . . .6D 23   SH 630 585
Cwm-coch . . . . . .3D 23   SH 634 613
Cwm Croesor . . . .3E 61   SH 641 453
Cwm Du . . . . . . .4F 31   SH 536 555
Cwm Dudodyn . . . .4B 22   SH 613 604
Cwm Dwyfor . . . . .3A 44   SH 540 508
Cwm Dwythwch . . .2C 32   SH 568 574
Cwm Dyli . . . . . . .5D 35   SH 635 543
Cwm Edno . . . . . .2A 48   SH 667 510
Cwm Eigiau . . . . . .1E 25   SH 709 634
. . . . .6D 17   SH 692 641
Cwm Fynhadog Uchaf . . . .3C 48   SH 685 502
Cwm Gafr . . . . . . .5B 22   SH 617 594
Cwm Gern Gof . . . .5C 24   SH 681 590
Cwm Glas . . . . . . .4B 34   SH 613 555
Cwm Glas Bach . . . .3A 34   SH 609 564
Cwmglas Bach . . . .1A 24   SH 662 638
Cwm Glas Crafnant
    National Nature Reserve
. . . . .5B 26   SH 735 598
Cwmglas Mawr . . . .1A 24   SH 667 634
Cwm Glas Mawr . . .3B 34   SH 618 562
Cwm Hafodyredwydd . .2E 65   SH 766 469
Cwm Idwal
    National Nature Reserve
. . . . .5E 23   SH 641 593
Cwm Llan . . . . . . .1B 46   SH 615 521
Cwm Llefrith . . . . .2A 58   SH 545 466
Cwm Lloer . . . . . . .2A 24   SH 661 622
Cwm Llugwy . . . . . .1C 24   SH 687 631
Cwm Marchnad . . .2B 44   SH 556 519
Cwm Meillionen . . . .5C 44   SH 561 483
Cwm Merch . . . . . .1D 47   SH 631 521
Cwm Padrig . . . . . .1C 34   SH 623 580
Cwm Pen-llafar . . . .6F 15   SH 657 645
Cwm Penmachno . .1D 65   SH 751 473
Cwm Pennant . . . .1F 57   SH 532 474
Cwm Perfedd . . . .3C 22   SH 628 619
Cwm Tal-y-braich . .3E 25   SH 705 617
Cwm Teigl . . . . . . .4A 64   SH 728 442
Cwm Tregalan . . . .6B 34   SH 611 534
Cwm Treweunydd . .5E 33   SH 584 546
Cwm Trwsgl . . . . . .4A 44   SH 547 494
Cwm Tryfan . . . . . .6A 24   SH 668 589
Cwm Uchaf . . . . . .4C 34   SH 621 553

Cwm y Caseg-fraith . .2B 36   SH 671 577
Cwmyffynnon . . . . .1F 43   SH 537 520
Cwm-y-glo . . . . . .2B 20   SH 551 626
Cwm-yr-haf . . . . . .2B 56   SH 492 467
Cwm yr Hafod . . . .2C 32   SH 561 576
Dduallt Halt . . . . . .6B 62   SH 678 421
Deganwy . . . . . . .2F 7   SH 777 793
Deganwy Station . . . .2F 7   SH 779 790
Deiniolen . . . . . . .1D 21   SH 575 630
Derlwyn . . . . .6E 21   SH 588 586
Devil's Kitchen . . . .6D 23   SH 638 588
Dinas Bach . . . . . .3D 35   SH 631 560
Dinas Mawr . . . . . .6C 40   SH 808 539
Dinas Mot . . . . . . .3C 34   SH 625 562
Dinas y Gromlech . . .3C 34   SH 629 569
Dinorwig . . . . . . .3E 21   SH 586 617
Dolbadarn Castle . . .5E 21   SH 585 598
Dolbenmaen . . . . .5C 56   SH 506 430
Dolgarrog . . . . . . .3E 19   SH 769 674
Dolwyddelan . . . . .1B 50   SH 736 522
Dolwyddelan Castle Car Park
. . . . .1A 50   SH 722 521
Dolwyddelan Station . .1B 50   SH 737 521
Drosgl . . . . .3A 16   SH 663 679
Drum . . . . .6E 11   SH 708 695
Drws Gwyn . . . . . .6B 28   SH 796 589
Drws-y-coed . . . . .6A 32   SH 541 534
Dulyn Reservoir . . . .4E 17   SH 700 665
Dwygyfylchi . . . . . .4B 6   SH 734 772
Dyffryn Conwy . . . .5F 53   SH 834 486
Dyffryn Mymbyr . . . .3C 36   SH 683 563
Dyffryn Nantlle . . . .6E 31   SH 522 530
Elidir Fach . . . . . . .3A 22   SH 603 613
Elidir Fawr . . . . . . .3B 22   SH 611 613
Esgair Felen . . . . .2D 35   SH 633 577
Esgair y Ceunannt . . .5B 22   SH 616 598
Fachwen . . . . . . .3D 21   SH 571 618
Fairy Glen . . . . . . .5C 40   SH 801 541
Ffestiniog Railway . . .2C 68   SH 626 405
. . . . .3C 62   SH 688 452
Ffridd y Bwlch . . . . .5E 49   SH 700 480
Ffynnon Caseg . . . .6B 16   SH 678 649
Ffynnon Lloer . . . . .2A 24   SH 662 621
Ffynnon Llugwy Reservoir
. . . . .2D 25   SH 692 627
Ffynnon Llyffant . . . .6C 16   SH 688 645
Foel Boeth . . . . . .6C 52   SH 804 478
Foel Boethwel . . . .6F 47   SH 651 477
Foel Ddu . . . . . . .2A 62   SH 669 460
. . . . .6D 53   SH 814 475
Foel Dduarth . . . . .4C 10   SH 681 714
Foel Felen . . . . . . .1E 51   SH 761 528
Foel-fras . . . . .5A 50   SH 727 481
. . . . .2D 17   SH 696 681
Foel-ganol . . . . . . .4C 10   SH 688 715
Foel Ganol . . . . . . .5A 16   SH 666 654
Foel-goch . . . . . . .3C 22   SH 628 611
Foel Goch . . . . . . .3D 33   SH 570 563
. . . . .2B 48   SH 677 513
Foel Grach . . . . . .5C 16   SH 688 658
Foelgraig . . . . .1F 23   SH 653 637
Foel Gron . . . . . . .3C 32   SH 563 565
Foel Lûs . . . . .5B 6   SH 732 761
Foel Lwyd . . . . . . .3A 12   SH 720 723
. . . . .1F 17   SH 713 693
Foel Meirch . . . . . .1F 23   SH 658 633
Foel Rudd . . . . . . .3E 65   SH 760 450
. . . . .5A 32   SH 548 543
Gallt Cedryn . . . . .2F 25   SH 713 629
Gallt-y-foel . . . . . .2E 21   SH 582 624
Gallt y Pandy . . . . .6C 40   SH 802 536
Gallt yr Ogof . . . . .6C 24   SH 685 585
Gallt y Wenallt . . . .6E 35   SH 642 532
Garndolbenmaen . .4B 56   SH 497 441
Garnedd-goch . . . .4D 43   SH 511 495
Garnedd Ugain . . . .4B 34   SH 611 551
Garn Prys . . . . . . .5E 55   SH 887 483
Garreg . . . . .1B 68   SH 612 416
Garreg Fawr . . . . . .2D 11   SH 690 730
Garreg Wastad . . . .2C 34   SH 625 571
Garth . . . . .5C 66   SH 566 378
Gellilydan . . . . . . .3C 70   SH 684 397
Gerlan . . . . .4D 15   SH 632 664
Gilfach Ddu Station . .4E 21   SH 585 604
Gladstone Rock . . . .1B 46   SH 618 523
Glan Conwy . . . . . .1F 53   SH 833 520
Glan Dwyfach . . . . .5A 56   SH 485 434
Glan Llugwy . . . . . .3C 24   SH 684 612
Glan y Môr Elias Nature Reserve
. . . . .1A 10   SH 667 743
Glasgwm . . . . . . .3F 51   SH 774 502
Glaslyn . . . . .5B 34   SH 617 545
Glastraeth . . . . . . .6A 68   SH 605 365

Gledrffordd . . . . . . .6E 17   SH 703 648
Glyder Fâch . . . . . . .1F 35   SH 656 582
Glyder Fawr . . . . . .2E 35   SH 642 579
Glyn Lledr . . . . . . .6A 40   SH 783 537
Golan . . . . .6E 57   SH 524 426
Gors Graianog . . . .3B 56   SH 495 453
Graig Cwm Dulyn . .4B 42   SH 496 491
Graig Ddû . . . . . . .2B 34   SH 619 574
Graig Goch . . . . . .4D 65   SH 751 443
Graig-las . . . . .4E 43   SH 520 495
Graig-lwyd . . . . . . .2D 57   SH 514 468
Graig Lwyd . . . . . .3B 26   SH 733 610
Graig Wen . . . . . . .4E 51   SH 763 490
Grib Ddu . . . . .5A 46   SH 606 482
Grinllwm . . . . .2F 27   SH 776 624
Groesffordd . . . . . .6E 7   SH 768 759
Gwaith Powdwr Nature Reserve
. . . . .4C 68   SH 620 389
Gwastadannas . . . .6F 35   SH 657 536
Gwastadnant . . . . .2B 34   SH 611 578
Gwaun y Garnedd . .5C 16   SH 687 652
Gwastad Castle . . . .3B 28   SH 796 610
Gwydir Uchaf Chapel . .4B 28   SH 794 609
Gwydir Uchaf Car Park
. . . . .4B 28   SH 795 608
Gyffin . . . . .5F 7   SH 777 768
Gyrn . . . . .2E 15   SH 647 688
Gyrn Lâs . . . . .4B 34   SH 611 558
Gyrn Wigau . . . . . .3F 15   SH 654 674
Hafna Mine Car Park . . . .4A 28   SH 781 601
Hafod Garregog
    National Nature Reserve
. . . . .4A 60   SH 602 444
Hafodyredwydd . . . .3E 65   SH 765 457
Halfway Bridge . . . .2A 14   SH 607 689
Halfway House . . . .3F 33   SH 599 569
Halfway Station . . . .2F 33   SH 597 574
Hebron Station . . . .1E 33   SH 583 584
Hendre . . . . .5F 7   SH 771 764
Henryd . . . . .1F 13   SH 770 747
Hir Ynys . . . . .2A 68   SH 604 404
Hwylfa . . . . .2D 53   SH 817 511
Idwal Cottage Youth Hostel
. . . . .4E 23   SH 648 603
Iolyn Park . . . . . . .6F 7   SH 774 753
Ivy Bridge . . . . . . .3F 69   SH 654 394
Iwerddon . . . . . . .1A 52   SH 788 525
Lavan Sands . . . . . .1C 8   SH 628 747
Lion Rock . . . . . . .3D 45   SH 576 500
Llanbedr-y-cennin . . .1E 19   SH 760 694
Llanberis . . . . .4D 21   SH 577 604
Llanberis Lake Railway . .3D 21   SH 571 615
Llanberis Path . . . . .2F 33   SH 597 572
Llanberis Station
    (Llanberis Lake Railway)
. . . . .5E 21   SH 582 599
Llanberis Station
    (Snowdon Mountain Railway)
. . . . .5E 21   SH 582 597
Llanberis Youth Hostel . .5D 21   SH 574 596
Llanddoged . . . . . .1C 28   SH 806 637
Llandecwyn . . . . . .5D 69   SH 632 375
Llandecwyn Station . .5B 68   SH 618 379
Llandygai . . . . . . .5A 8   SH 599 708
Llanfairfechan . . . . .1C 10   SH 682 747
Llan Ffestiniog . . . .1E 71   SH 702 419
Llanfihangel-y-pennant . .4E 57   SH 526 448
Llanfrothen . . . . . .1C 68   SH 622 412
Llangelynin . . . . . .2F 13   SH 771 735
Llanllechid . . . . . . .2C 14   SH 623 686
Llanrhychwyn . . . . .3F 27   SH 775 616
Llanrwst . . . . .3B 28   SH 798 616
Llanrwst Station . . . .3C 28   SH 800 617
Llechog . . . . .3A 34   SH 604 568
. . . . .6F 33   SH 598 536
Llechwedd . . . . . .5E 7   SH 760 760
Llechwedd Garnedd . .5C 36   SH 685 541
Llechwedd Mawr . .5F 65   SH 779 435
Llechwedd Oernant . .6A 52   SH 788 478
Llechwedd Slate Caverns
. . . . .1E 63   SH 700 471
Llefn . . . . .2E 15   SH 640 685
Llethr Gwyn . . . . . .3A 26   SH 724 610
Llewedd Bach . . . .6C 34   SH 627 532
Llwyd Mawr . . . . . .2C 56   SH 503 461
Llwytmor . . . . .1C 16   SH 688 692
Llwytmor Bach . . . .6C 10   SH 680 699
Llyn Anafon . . . . . .6D 11   SH 698 698
Llyn Bach . . . . .4B 34   SH 615 555
Llyn Bochlwyd . . . .5F 23   SH 654 592
Llyn Bodgynydd . . . .5E 27   SH 760 592
Llyn Bowydd . . . . .2A 64   SH 725 462
Llyn Bychan . . . . . .5D 27   SH 751 593

Safety & Security when walking

GENERAL

◆ Make sure you are wearing appropriate clothing and footwear, with suitable extra clothing in case the weather changes, or if you get delayed or misjudge how long it will take you to complete the walk.
◆ Be careful, if you are inexperienced, not to undertake a walk that is too ambitious.
◆ Take plenty to eat and drink, there are not always opportunities to buy extra provisions.
◆ Be sure someone knows where you are going and when to expect you back. Let them know when you have returned as well.
◆ Although taking a mobile phone is a good idea, in some remote areas there may not be a signal and therefore should not be relied upon.
◆ When walking on roads follow the advice in the Highway Code.
◆ Always use a pavement and safe crossing points whenever possible.
◆ Where there is no pavement it is better to walk on the right hand side of the road, facing oncoming traffic.
◆ Only cross railway lines at designated places and never walk along railway lines.

MOUNTAIN WALKING

Every year visitors to mountainous regions are killed or injured either because they have gone without appropriate clothing and equipment, or that the conditions had been severely underestimated. A mountain top can be icy cold on a summer's day, and weather conditions can change very quickly. Do not venture on to the mountains unless you are properly equipped and have thoroughly checked weather forecasts in advance, particularly those detailing local conditions.

◆ Good navigational skills and a compass are essential.
◆ Always take warm and waterproof clothing; conditions higher up a mountain can be very different to those at the bottom, even in summer.
◆ Walking boots should always be worn.
◆ Gloves and headgear are advisable too in cold weather.
◆ Other essentials to take are; a waterproof backpack, "high energy" foods, a whistle, a torch (with spare batteries and bulb), a watch, a first aid kit, water purification tablets and a survival bag.
◆ Ready made first aid kits are available with all necessary items included.
◆ High factor sunscreen should be used in sunny weather, the sun can be particularly strong higher up mountains, even in winter. Sunglasses or goggles are advisable too.

The international distress signal is six blasts of a whistle repeated at one minute intervals (the reply is three) or six flashes of light at one minute intervals (again the reply is three). Mountain Rescue should only be called in cases of a real emergency by dialling 999 (all phones) or 112 (mobiles only) and asking for "police" and then "mountain rescue".

THE COUNTRY CODE

◆ Be safe - plan ahead and follow any signs.
Even when going out locally, it's best to get the latest information about where and when you can go; for example, your rights to go onto some areas of open land may be restricted while work is carried out, for safety reasons or during breeding seasons. Follow advice and local signs, and be prepared for the unexpected.
◆ Leave gates and property as you find them.
Please respect the working life of the countryside, as our actions can affect people's livelihoods, our heritage, and the safety and welfare of animals and ourselves.
◆ Protect plants and animals, and take your litter home.
We have a responsibility to protect our countryside now and for future generations, so make sure you don't harm animals, birds, plants, or trees. Fires can be as devastating to wildlife and habitats as they are to people and property.
◆ Keep dogs under close control.
The countryside is a great place to exercise dogs, but it's every owner's duty to make sure their dog is not a danger or nuisance to farm animals, wildlife or other people.
◆ Consider other people.
Showing consideration and respect for other people makes the countryside a pleasant environment for everyone - at home, at work and at leisure.